THE VISUAL SYSTEM of WORK

Help Your Business Work Better,
Make Money and Generate Cash:
A 90 Day Implementation Guide

First Revised Edition

David T. Lord

David T. Lord Consulting, LLC

THE VISUAL SYSTEM of WORK

Help Your Business Work Better,
Make Money and Generate Cash:
A 90-Day Implementation Guide

This edition published by

David T. Lord Consulting, LLC
PO Box 971334
Ypsilanti, MI 48197
david@davidtlord.com

First Revised Edition

Library of Congress Control Number: 2013913587

International Standard Book Number
ISBN-13: 978-0-9797645-0-9

Book Design: Joshua Smith and Jessica Janda

Book Cover Design: Jerry Hutchinson

Editor: Lolo A. Lord

Photography: David T. Lord

Printed in the United States of America.

In Memory

My father, mentor and friend

TRACY E. LORD

1927-2007
_____

"Few things are more strategic than organizational capabilities. Competitors can match or trump capital, marketing campaigns or new products and services. But few competitors have the foresight, discipline and skill to build a strong and constantly improving organization."

— *Jim Clemmer*, *leadership, change, team, and organization effectiveness author and speaker*

Table of Contents
TC

FOREWORD

Much is written about strategy, but very little about how to implement that strategy. We have all been carried away by grand strategic plans, only to revisit those plans a year later to see that nothing has changed and nothing has been implemented. This book changes all that...effective execution of a business strategy is at its heart. *The Visual System of Work* provides a method and tools to help an organization work better, make money and generate cash...in other words, to be successful.

I have had the pleasure of working with David over the past 15 years on various projects and initiatives in private, educational and non-profit organizations and have always found him to bring value to any dialog with his holistic thinking and process analysis skills. He is an excellent communicator, encourager and problem-solver and knows how to create order out of chaos. David understands the challenges of running a small business, using dialog, data and visual management tools to help organizations see and accept their current reality.

The Visual System of Work identifies tools to bring about long-term organizational improvement versus simply focusing on the episodic. This book will help the reader answer the question, "What's important?" for his or her organization. Adopting the "8 Tools" will quickly enable an organization to chart its path to continuous improvement and long-term success.

David's deep understanding of process analysis and the importance of the right metrics unlock the secrets to thriving as a small business in an ever turbulent, ever changing world. His book will bring value to any who possess the desire, drive and discipline to win in the game of business. *The Visual System of Work* will quickly become one of the most treasured books in your business library.

Now, begin your journey to excellence and making the world a better place. Good reading...

Craig Schrotenboer
Vice President of Operations
KIDS HOPE USA

Introduction
In
Making Work Visible

"Work is love made visible. And if you can't work with love, but only with distaste, it is better that you should leave your work and sit at the gate of the temple and take alms of the people who work with joy."

— *Kahlil Gibran,* a Lebanese-American artist, poet, and writer

INTRODUCTION

Making Work Visible

Twenty years ago, while working as a small business consultant, I discovered an ingeniously simple method for helping a business get better. The method's concepts are simple, easy to implement and can be used on any size or kind of business.

The method, making work visible, uses simple visualization as a vehicle for understanding complex business structure. The simple act of seeing how a business works naturally leads employees to more personal involvement as well as better communication, cooperation and coordination of effort within that business.

When employees can see the interconnections within an organization they have the information they need to work together as a cohesive unit...and that transforms a business.

This method continues to work over time, even when you take into account all the changes and renovations that will naturally take place in every business. Often, when I go back and check in with businesses that I had once helped make better, I find that they are still using the same visual tools and methods I had once showed them. Those are also the businesses that continue to get better, make money and generate cash.

When I see that kind of progress, it is my greatest reward. As a business consultant, my goal is to take a business from the depths of economic uncertainty to the heights of financial security. It would give me great pleasure if you, too, decided to take your business on that journey. By applying the method and tools in this book, your company will soon be working better, having happier employees, and more loyal customers and, most importantly, making more money and generating more cash.

Underlying Assumptions

1. Every business has opportunities for improvement.

2. Identifying and improving those areas will help the business work better.

3. When actual observation and concrete data are used to evaluate the business (rather than relying on people's perceptions) solutions emerge to help the business work better

4. All members of the business must collaborate to analyze data and generate solutions for improving performance.

5. When involved, everyone within the business will help to improve performance.

Chapter 01
What Are Your Core Values?

"When a company has a strong set of core values it will drive all critical business decisions. Employees will become engaged and will take pride in how they do their work. The organization will attract and retain top talent. Core values create their own ROI (Return On Investment)."

— *Deborah Siday,* Money Management International, commenting on the *The Importance of Core Values*

01

WHAT ARE YOUR CORE VALUES?

Business Transformation

Transforming an organization takes more than just transmitting ideas. It requires an understanding of what actually goes on in the business. Transforming a business means changing values through education with the objective of improving the organization's effectiveness.

The first step is to facilitate an understanding of how an organization is presently working. The solutions to many problems become evident as soon as they are seen and discovered. The business leadership can then help the organization work together to find solutions by promoting employee involvement. An organization succeeds when it uses its own resources effectively and its employees contribute to process improvement. When people are involved in improving the business, they accept and use the solutions they generate.

The more knowledge people have about a company, the better that company will perform. You will always be more successful in business by sharing information with the people you work with than by keeping them in the dark. Open-book management is the practice of communicating with people via the numbers. This must become the cornerstone of running your small business. Once employees understand the numbers, they understand how their efforts affect the company and changes their motivation for working.

People: The Most Important Asset

"Offering employees a say in the decisions that affect them is one of the best tools for engaging their hearts, minds and souls so they are motivated to give their all—and to make better choices as a company."

—**Verne Harnsish,** *Founder and CEO of Gazelles and author of Mastering the Rockefeller Habits and Michael Synk, founder of In-Synk and Gazelles coach*

People perform best when they are appreciated and feel like they belong. Unfortunately, many business owners don't think about the atmosphere that exists in their workplace until a problem occurs—the work isn't getting done or an employee survey shows that employees are unhappy.

The culture of a business can influence employee motivation by creating an environment that allows employees to feel appreciated; free to express their ideas and know that they will be treated fairly.

01

What Are Your Core Values?

"It's not hard to make decisions when you know what your values are."

— **Roy Disney,** *an American businessman, who, along with his younger brother Walt Disney, co-founded, what is now The Walt Disney Company*

What does your business stand for? What are the core values of your organization? Does your business offer any underlying purpose for your employees to come in and perform each day?

Core Values is one of those business terms that has been so overused and misunderstood that we often dismiss it. Jim Collins and Jerry Porras discussed core values in *Built to Last*, identifying that all great companies had a clear set of core values. In the years following their book, many companies developed and announced their core values with much fanfare, only to see little impact on the organization. They were not actually used for anything, and employees observed leadership not living according to the values or demanding them in their people and organization.

What are core values?

Core values are a small set of essential and timeless guiding principles for your company. They are what define your culture and guide all of your actions.

What is the greatest benefit to identifying your core values?

Core values define your unique culture and who you are as people. When they are defined and rigorously adhered to throughout your business by everyone, a thriving culture will grow with these core values at the center.

Why put core values first?

It's simple. If someone doesn't care about or value what you value, they should not be working in the business. They will ruin the company's journey for everyone else. Whatever core values you choose, you must be committed to them and be willing to live by them.

In his book *Good to Great*, Jim Collins recommends that every organization needs to get the right people in the right seats on the bus. Who are the "right people"? Quite simply, they are people who exhibit your core values, regardless of their knowledge, technical skills or experience.

Chapter
02
Why Small Business Matters in America

"If you ask me to name the proudest distinction of Americans, I would choose – because it contains all the others – the fact that they were the people who created the phrase 'to make money'. No other language or nation had ever used these words before; men had always thought of wealth as a static quantity – to be seized, begged, inherited, shared, looted, or obtained as a favor. Americans were the first to understand that wealth has to be created. The words 'to make money' hold the essence of human morality."

— *Francisco D'Anconia,* one of the central characters in *Atlas Shrugged,* in which he was the owner by inheritance of the world's largest copper mining empire

02

WHY SMALL BUSINESS MATTERS IN AMERICA

The Key to Economic Growth

"That great phrase — 'a rising tide lifts all boats' — was coined by the late Jack Kemp, who believed that growth and opportunity for all is the answer to poverty. In fact, Kemp believed it was the answer to all things economic. And he was right. The best anti-poverty program is the one that creates jobs. The answer to large budget deficits? Grow the economy, create jobs, watch incomes rise, and let the tax revenues come rolling in."

— *Lawrence Kudlow, conservative economist, television personality, and newspaper columnist*

The Velocity of Money

The term "velocity of money" describes the average number of times money is spent on new goods and services within an allotted period of time. When money circulates, the economy grows. When money doesn't circulate, the economy becomes sluggish and fails. In order to have a vigorous economy, money has to stay in motion and the faster it moves, the healthier the economy will be.

A small amount of money can fund a large number of purchases when it circulates at a fast pace. Small businesses have the ability to circulate money faster than large ones. That is why, when you stimulate the economy of small companies, you stimulate the larger, general economy as well.

Small businesses that have the foresight, discipline and skill to build strong and constantly improving organizations, are the ones that create a smooth, steady and constant flow of work that help the business grow, take care of customers, make money and generate cash.

When small businesses have the organizational capability to perform well by increasing the speed of work flowing through the business, the velocity of money will increase and all people benefit.

02

The Importance of Small Business to the US Economy

Never underestimate the enormous impact of small businesses on the wealth of our nation. While many people in the United States think that large businesses are the most important factor in driving the economy, small business employs over half of the country's workforce. Small business is what stimulates economic growth.

The importance of small businesses to the United States overall economy has never been so evident. The following infographics illustrate the great contributions that small businesses make to the economy of the United States and to the world.

1. The latest figures show that small businesses create 75 percent of the net new jobs in our economy.

2. Small businesses make up 97 percent of exporters and produce 29 percent of all export value.

3. Small patenting firms produce 13 to 14 times more patents per employee than large patenting firms.

4. Small businesses make up more than 99.7% of all employers.

Source: **U.S. Small Business Administration**

Latest figures show that
SMALL BUSINESSES
CREATE
75%
of the net new jobs in our economy.

SMALL BUSINESSES
—— make up to ——
97%
——of exporters——
& produce
29%
of all export value

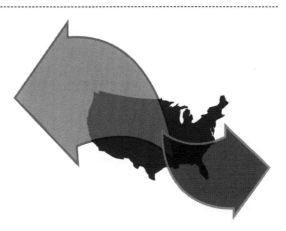

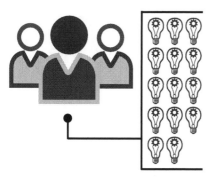

SMALL PATENTING FIRMS PRODUCE
13-14 TIMES
more patents per employee than large patenting firms

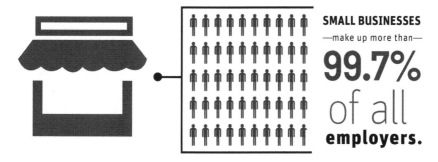

SMALL BUSINESSES
—make up more than—
99.7%
of all
employers.

Chapter
03
The Challenge for a Small Business Owner

"It takes a lot of courage to start a small business. It takes even more courage to stick with it during tough times like these when the nation's financial structure is wobbling, uncertainty fills the air and even the basic principles of free enterprise are being questioned by anti-business politicians."

— *Dan Danner,* President and CEO, National Federation of Independent Business (NFIB)

03

THE CHALLENGE FOR A SMALL BUSINESS OWNER

Strength in the Face of Pain

Owning a business can be unusually painful. If you are like most business owners, you're busy running your business without always knowing what's really going on and who's really doing what. That can lead to 'putting out fires' and dealing with complaints, criticism and condemnation in the workplace...not productive and not fun.

If you see this happening at your company, something needs to change. A successful business owner needs to have communication, cooperation and coordination of effort for the business to grow and stay competitive. Transformation comes when sharing information and shared decision-making are the norm. If you want to change from "being in the dark" to knowing what is going on, create a work environment where everyone speaks a common language and is committed to improving the way work is done.

A business has to make money and generate cash in order to exist. To do that, the business has to either save money (lower costs) or increase throughput (see page 45). Businesses often choose the "save money" mindset even though the overwhelming evidence says that "generating money" is a much better option. An important step in shifting a company's focus from costs to throughput is to develop a strategy.

Once a company develops and communicates the strategy, its employees will better understand which activities should be improved first and how they can assist in the effort. The strategy enables development of a systematic process for continual improvement. In order to develop a strategy, a business owner needs to understand what's most important.

Developing a Strategy

The word "strategy" comes from the Greek word for "generalship". Like a good general, strategies give overall direction for an initiative. How are you going to win as your business moves forward? That's the key question behind developing strategy. To win at anything worthwhile, you need a game plan. To be successful means knowing how to use your employees and resources to best advantage, and it's very difficult to "win" if you don't have a strategic game plan in place.

Analyzing sales data for making strategic decisions

"Our company initially retained David solely to lead a one-day executive retreat. We were growing and doing well, and at the same time, we knew there were many opportunities to improve. During our short retreat, David helped us define the core areas that would require the greatest focus over the next six months, as well as the key actions we would need to take to drive longer-term and sustainable improvement. As a leadership team, we found such value from our time with David that we expanded that initial engagement from one day to well over a year."

— *Joe Hart, President, Asset Health*

Chapter
04
You Can't Manage What You Can't See

"One picture is worth
ten thousand words."

— *Chinese Proverb*

04

YOU CAN'T MANAGE WHAT YOU CAN'T SEE

A System Thinking Approach to Running a Business

"Ideally, wisdom is total perspective -- seeing an object, event, or idea in all its pertinent relationships. Spinoza defined wisdom as seeing things sub specie eternitatis, in view of eternity; I suggest defining it as seeing things sub specie totius, in view of the whole."

— **Will Durant,** prolific American writer, historian, and philosopher

Interconnectedness means looking at the organization as a whole. It starts with the basic belief that every function within an organization is connected to everything else. By thinking in terms of systems, businesses get a better picture of the relationships between its parts, rather than just seeing the parts themselves. Businesses then have a better perspective for defining (and achieving) the actions that maximize both individual and organizational success. The overall effectiveness of a business improves dramatically when the entire system is examined, rather than just the individual parts.

Overcoming Business Silo Mentality

"The silo mentality, in a nutshell, is a business approach where each worker looks out for his or her department and not the company. When 'what's in it for me and my department' surpasses what's best for the company, everyone suffers."

— **Gary M. Stern,** *New York-based freelance writer and co-author of Minority Rules: Turn Your Ethnicity into a Competitive Edge*

Silo mentality is when a competitive structure and lack of communication prevents several departments or groups in an organization from sharing information or knowledge with others in the same company. A silo mentality reduces effectiveness and contributes to a failing corporate culture. Silo mentality leads to redundancies, poor communication, reduced trust and often pits one department or group against another.

Competition within a business prevents positive results. The silo approach (where a business measures each function independently) focuses on improving efficiency within each individual silo. This makes it nearly impossible to pay attention to the leverage point where all areas of the business work together for the common good. A simple and effective framework to align every part of a business can remove silo mentality.

04

Making Work Visible

"A visual workplace is a work environment that is self-explaining, self-regulating, and self-improving, where what is supposed to happen does happen, on time, every time, night or day."

— **Gwendolyn D. Galsworth,** founder and President of Quality Methods International and the Visual-Lean® Institute (QMI)

The way business works is not always apparent. Too often, workers make assumptions about how tasks are performed. By making work visible, employees have a shared view of the workplace. When employees see how the business works, they can discuss ideas on how to improve the performance of the business. Making work visible provides a mechanism for continuous improvement through system alignment and goal clarity. It helps to engage people in the process and improve communication and information sharing throughout the organization.

Breaking Down Your Business

Visualization is a catalyst for obtaining system understanding. To visualize your business, you need to think about it in a structured way. Making work visible leads to personal involvement, communication, cooperation and coordination of effort as everyone feels part of the whole system.

Discussing workflow constraints

"The Visual System of Work helps you have the ability to break down every aspect of your business into its basic elements. Once you do that, you can measure and track what is happening every day. It is an eye opening experience to learn how your business really works compared to how you think it works."

— *Vincent Hazen, COO and General Counsel, LoneStar Logos & Signs.*

04 Visual Management

"First, visual management ensures the organization's internal structure, management systems, work environment, and culture are aligned with its mission and values. Second, it focuses employees' attention on critical goals, making sure that the employees know what is expected of them at all times and are committed to success."

— Stewart Liff and Pamela A. Posey, authors of Seeing is Believing: How The New Art Of Visual Management Can Boost Performance Throughout Your Organization

Visual Management is the practice of using information visualization techniques to manage work. The impact that visuals can have on quality, on-time delivery, cost and productivity is truly enormous. It helps create an environment that enhances employee commitment to the success of the organization by ensuring that the work environment and culture directly support the core values of that organization.

Visual Management provides a structure for on-going business improvement through goal clarity, system alignment, improved communication and information sharing throughout the organization and engagement of people in the business.

Discovering the best way to work together

The Benefits of Visual Management

Visual Management helps employees understand their influence on the organization's overall performance by seeing the business in its entirety. It motivates everybody to improve by clarifying key performance objectives and builds participation through shared information.

Visual Management increases the rate of work flowing through a business by simplifying and improving the delivery of on-time, complete and accurate information throughout the organization.

A Visual System of Work for a tubing manufacturer

"During a period of 8 months, working together as a team, including management and shop floor personnel, The Visual System of Work opened up our operation of activity like I have never seen before. David helped us quickly define and create our "System of Work" with work instructions and support procedure guidelines. We felt important as we progressed as a team."

— *James P. Millett, President, Tube Co.*

Chapter
05
What's Most Important?

"The only way to be secure is to make money and generate cash. Everything else is a means to that end."

— **Jack Stack,** founder and CEO of SRC Holdings, a company comprising more than 25 separate companies and author of two books, *The Great Game of Business* and *A Stake in the Outcome*

05

![black bar] **WHAT'S MOST IMPORTANT?**

Tracking, Monitoring and Keeping Score

"What gets measured gets improved."

— **Robin Sharma,** *a premier thinker on leadership, personal growth and life management and author of The Greatest Guide: Powerful Secrets for Getting to World Class*

The sharing of financial information with employees and helping them understand how their work affects the numbers is vital for a business to make money and generate cash. Having a process to track, monitor and keep score will assist employees to communicate with one another the day-to-day activities that have the greatest impact on whether the business is winning or losing. Rewarding employees for attaining positive outcomes will provide the incentive to keep everyone involved and focused on achieving success for the business.

Knowing the critical number that greatly influences the performance of a business is the challenge. A critical number is the number that employees must achieve in order for the business to succeed. The critical number might be how many units need to be produced to keep up with demand. It could be the number of sales or phone calls that need to be made.

How do you determine which measure is critical and which numbers will have the greatest impact to make money and generate cash? The answer lies in knowing the difference between Lag and Lead measures.

Lag and Lead Measures

"Using only lagging indicators in your business is very much like trying to drive your car using only the rearview or side mirrors. It's great for backing out of the driveway. Moving forward is difficult if not impossible."

— **Douglas Wick,** founder of Positioning Systems, which provides small businesses with the tools to make them more successful

Lag measures quantify the actual end results. The challenge with a Lag measure is that you are measuring the end result, something that you cannot control. For example, if you want to lose weight, you can step on a scale to measure your weight (Lag measure). In order to gain or lose weight, you will need to track and measure calorie intake and how many calories are being burned (Lead measures). To improve your weight, you should observe the Lead measure, a calculation that directly influences the Lag measure. **In other words, a Lead measure is something you can control in the moment; a Lag measure reflects something that has already happened.**

05

The Language of Business: The 3 Key Lag Measures

The language of business is money and the value of a business, in the long run, depends on its financial performance. Therefore, it is critical that all employees understand how their work impacts the company's financial health.

Over time, a business must bring in more money than it spends and have cash in-hand to run the business in doing so. The purpose of this chapter is to understand the key Lag and Lead measures in their simplest terms and how the Lead measures impact the Lag measures.

The first two key Lag measures communicate if the business is (1) making money and (2) generating cash. The first measure, Net Profit (NP), is shown on the Income Statement and the second measure, Cash Flow (CF), is shown on the Cash Flow Statement. When making money (Net Profit) and generating cash (Cash Flow) trends in a positive direction over time, the third key Lag measure, Equity (Assets/Liability) ($), shown on the Balance Sheet, increases. See Diagram 3.1.

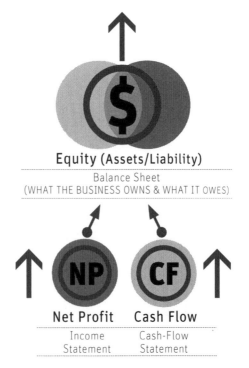

Equity (Assets/Liability)
Balance Sheet
(WHAT THE BUSINESS OWNS & WHAT IT OWES)

Net Profit   Cash Flow
Income   Cash-Flow
Statement   Statement

Diagram 3.1

The 3 Key Lead Measures

There are three key Lead measures for evaluating the impact of management decisions on small business performance:

1. Operating Expenses (OE) are the fixed costs in the period that a business will pay whether they sell something or not. All labor is included in OE and so is overtime.

2. True Variable Costs (TVC) include raw materials, sales commission, outside processing or subcontracted items and any other cost that is incurred as a result of a sale.

3. Throughput (T) is the rate at which a business generates money through sales.

See Diagram 3.2.

SYSTEM OF WORK

| OPERATING EXPENSES | TRUE VARIABLE COSTS | THROUGHPUT |

Diagram 3.2

05 How the 3 Lead Measures Impact the Bottom Line

The three Lead measures have a direct effect on the two Lag measures (Net Profit and Cash Flow.) When Throughput increases, there is a high likelihood that Net Profit and Cash Flow will increase. When Operating Expenses increase, there is a high likelihood that Net Profit and Cash Flow will decrease. You can see the relationship between all of the six measures in the following diagram, and how the three Lead measures impact the bottom line. See Diagram 3.3.

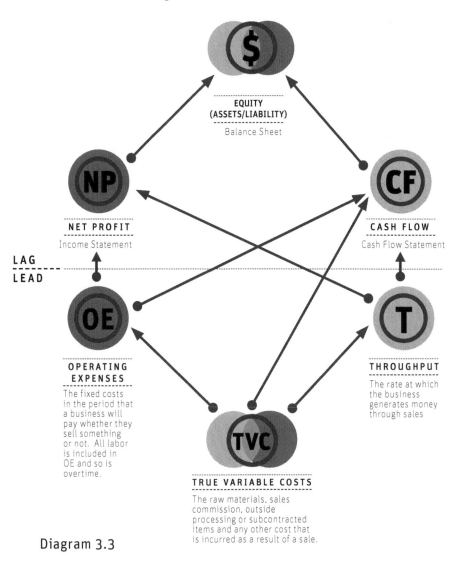

Diagram 3.3

The Importance of Smooth, Steady and Constant Workflow

"If you don't have time to do it right, when will you have time to do it over?"

— John Wooden, *an American basketball player and coach who won ten NCAA national championships in a 12-year period as head coach at UCLA*

A s you can see from Diagram 3.3, True Variable Costs is a Lead measure for Throughput and Operating Expenses.

Therefore, the rate that work flows through a business has the greatest impact on a small business to make money and generate cash.

A customer of any business expects on-time delivery of a quality (complete and accurate) product or service. On-time delivery depends on the capacity of the business and quality depends on the process and people capability of the business.

1. CAPACITY is the amount of products/services the overall business system can deliver on-time.

2. PROCESS CAPABILITY is the ability of the business processes to deliver complete and accurate products and services.

3. PEOPLE CAPABILITY is the ability of the business employees to complete their individual tasks completely and accurately.

What's most important?

Smooth, steady and constant workflow without interruptions...

A business must be capable and have the capacity to deliver on-time quality (accurate and complete) products or services to their customers while making money and generating cash. It is critical that all employees have the necessary skills to understand how their work (capability and capacity) impacts the company's financials.

Chapter 06
The Visual System of Work

"An organization behaves as a system, regardless of whether it is being managed as a system. If an organization is not being managed as a system, it is not being effectively managed."

— *Geary A. Rummler and Alan P. Brache,*
authors of *Improving Performance: How to Manage the White Space on the Organization Chart*

06

THE VISUAL SYSTEM OF WORK

Developing Trust

"Robert Shaw, has said, 'Above all, success in business requires two things: a winning competitive strategy and superb organization execution. Distrust is the enemy of both.' I submit that while high trust won't necessarily rescue a poor strategy, low trust will almost always derail a good one."

— **Stephen M. R. Covey,** co-founder and CEO of CoveyLink *Worldwide and author of The SPEED of Trust*

Businesses develop trust and productive relationships within their organizations by listening to the concerns and issues of employees and telling them the truth. When workers engage in honest and open dialog, they feel committed to their jobs, enthused about the future and motivated to come up with ideas that enhance the organization.

Creating real change within an organization requires collective effort, where everyone speaks a common language and is committed to improving the way work is done. Businesses arrive at answers when information is communicated freely and shared decision-making is the norm. Communication, cooperation and coordination of effort are needed for a business to grow and stay competitive in the marketplace.

Behavior Characteristics of a Reactive Workplace	**Behavior Characteristics of a Creative Workplace**
• Complaining	• Communication
• Criticizing	• Cooperation
• Condemning	• Coordination of Effort

Visual management enhances communication and accelerates project completion by representing situational relationships of data in a meaningful and informative story. People are enthusiastic about improving the enterprise when they can actually see how their individual actions affect the company's performance. By being aware of how employees adapt to change, businesses support acceptance of improvement initiatives and encourage shared decision-making.

Businesses that establish and maintain trust throughout their organizations create an environment where communication, cooperation and coordination of work are the norm. When employees have the proper tools and training, they become trusted "accountants," that is, employees who take responsibility to track, monitor and report on the businesses' ongoing performance.

06 Introduction to The Visual System of Work

"The hardest thing to explain is the glaring evidence which everybody had decided not to see."

— **Ayn Rand,** *a Russian-American novelist, philosopher, playwright, and screenwriter, known for her two best-selling novels, The Fountainhead and Atlas Shrugged*

The question I am asked most frequently by a small business owner who is interested in making their business better is, "Where should we start?" Given the complexity of issues and concerns, I tell my client: "Start by implementing The Visual System of Work."

In my work experience, that is the method that has had the greatest success in impact on team performance and ease of implementation. Quick and highly visible wins are critical to building momentum and gaining credibility for any improvement initiative. The Visual System of Work is, quite simply, the best place to begin your improvement transformation.

To begin The Visual System of Work we need two key foundations:

1. Storyboards

2. The War Room

Storyboards

A storyboard is a powerful medium for displaying and sharing information. This communication tool provides a framework for visualizing ideas, plans and activities. When people have something to look at, it is much easier to understand concepts, interpret diagrams or charts, and visualize the future. Using storyboards increases people's meaningful involvement and, in turn, that involvement dramatically enhances teamwork.

Storyboarding is a visual process used to display thinking. It is designed to bring out a group's best thinking and energy on a specific issue. Storyboarding can be used in brainstorming sessions, planning, problem solving, organizing, or just capturing thoughts.

A storyboard showing vital information for running a cabinetry installation business

A retailer's tracking/monitoring storyboard   A storyboard for a health care provider

06

The War Room

Because every business is in a competitive battle, it makes sense to have a designated war room (command center) with the best information available to guide decision-making. The walls of a war room are filled with storyboards that display charts, graphs and other information needed for running the business.

Something magical happens when you set up an entire meeting space as a visual environment. The war room is where business teams meet to review business performance and to have meaningful dialog for helping the business get better. It becomes a place for meetings that promote collaboration and keep the business running smoothly as well as a place for quickly addressing problems and issues to improve business performance.

A War Room for a manufacturing company

A War Room for a sales and distribution business

A War Room for a Department Manager

06

Introduction to the Tools

"... When our tools don't work, we tend to blame ourselves... When our tools are broken, we feel broken. And when somebody fixes one, we feel a tiny bit more whole."

— **Lev Grossman,** *American novelist, journalist and a senior writer and book critic for Time*

As stated earlier, the method, Making Work Visible, uses simple visualization as a vehicle for understanding complex business structure. The simple act of seeing how a business works naturally leads employees to more personal involvement as well as better communication, cooperation and coordination of effort within that business.

The following eight (8) tools help employees see the interconnections within the business and provide the information they need to work together to help the business get better, make money and generate cash.

The tools assist in documenting, analyzing, evaluating and reviewing on-going business performance. By combining the tools, small business owners and their employees are able to discover the best way to run their business.

Eight Tools for Helping Your Business Get Better

1. **The Strategic Planning Sheet**

2. **The Financial Sheet**

3. **The Functional Organization Structure Sheet**

4. **The System of Work Diagram**

5. **The Meeting Matrix Sheet**

6. **The (2) Time Management Sheets**

7. **The 5W-2H Worksheet**

8. **The Scoreboard Sheet**

Note: To introduce The Visual System of Work, I am sharing the method by presenting each tool with examples and photos. I hope this will help you, the reader, to grasp and understand the power of The Visual System of Work.

Tool #1: The Strategic Planning Sheet

What is the 'current reality' of the business?

Complete the Strategic Planning Sheet to understand your "current" business reality. When you reach a shared understanding of the Core Values, The 5-Year Plan, The One-Year Plan, The Three Questions and the 80/20 relationships, your business will then be in a better position to develop a strategic action plan that is believable and attainable.

1. What are your business core values?

2. What is your business currently doing that is good?

3. What is your business doing that it should be doing better?

4. What is your business not doing that it should be doing?

5. What are your 5-year goals?

6. What are your 1-year goals?

7. During the past 18 months, what 20% of the products or services that your business provided created 80% of your total sales?

8. During the past 18 months, what 20% of your customers were responsible for 80% of your business's total sales?

9. What business processes created 20% of the products or services that created 80% of your business's total sales?

The Strategic Planning Sheet

CORE VALUES

3-QUESTIONS

What is your business doing that is good?

What is your business doing that it should be doing better?

5-YEAR GOALS

What is your business not doing that it should be doing?

1-YEAR GOALS

WHAT 20% OF THE PRODUCTS/SERVICES CREATED 80% OF THE TOTAL SALES?

WHAT 20% OF CUSTOMERS WERE RESPONSIBLE FOR 80% OF TOTAL SALES?

WHAT PROCESSES CREATED 20% OF THE PROD/SVC THAT CREATED 80% SALES?

Kid's Hope USA team members presenting their 3-Questions...

prioritizing what's important...

and creating a strategic action plan

A work session at Kids Hope USA

"I love the use of visual management to help identify an organization's reality and drive continuous improvement. The focus on any project is to improve the way work gets done. The method focuses on process improvement and developing the right metrics to guide improvement efforts versus focusing on the episodic."

— *Craig Schrotenboer, Vice President of Operations, Kids Hope USA*

Prioritizing what's important during a strategic planning session at Suburban Aviation

Tool #2: The Financial Sheet

Is your business making money?

Good financial information is an extremely powerful tool. Information is needed to show whether the business is on track or not, and whether the company is really making money.

Complete the Financial Sheet to see if your business is making money now and in the future. The Financial Sheet is a simple way to track, monitor and show whether your business is making money.

The Financial Sheet

	JAN	FEB	MAR	APR	MAY	JUN	JUL	AUG	SEP	OCT	NOV	DEC	TOTALS
MONEY COMING IN													
THROUGHPUT SALES 1													
THROUGHPUT SALES 2													
THROUGHPUT SALES 3													
TOTALS													
MONEY GOING OUT													
OPERATING EXPENSES													
TRUE VARIABLE COSTS													
BANK LOANS/ DEBT													
OTHER													
TOTALS													
CASH FLOW													

A storyboard tracking monthly Throughput at RHK Technology

"David is an excellent facilitator, always allowing us to discover what needed to be improved and how to do so. It was David who drove us to establish a Leadership Team within the company and who implemented a Monthly Financial Review. The Monthly Financial Review was not only an examination of previous results, but also a forecast of upcoming activity.

David always made sure we had a plan to achieve our desired results. He worked with individuals to develop their skills so appropriate behavior ensued. I grew significantly in my ability to obtain information, identify key actions and implement change. All those who encountered David enhanced their skill set."

— *Michael Kloc, Chief Financial Officer, RHK Technology*

Tool #3: The Functional Organization Structure Sheet

W ho is responsible for what?

Create a Functional Organizational Structure Sheet showing the person that should be accountable for each role or key position in your business.

A functional organizational chart displays, in a graphic format, the roles of each position in the company and the name of the employee who fills the role. It organizes the positions within the company by the purpose of the job or position.

Each hierarchical level represents the structure of the organization that the company needs to operate effectively. Laying out the levels of the company in a functional organization chart, gives precise and clear roles to each department in the company and to each individual who works in that department. It allows the viewer to easily see the positions in the business and what specific purpose or function each area fulfills.

The Functional Organization Structure Sheet

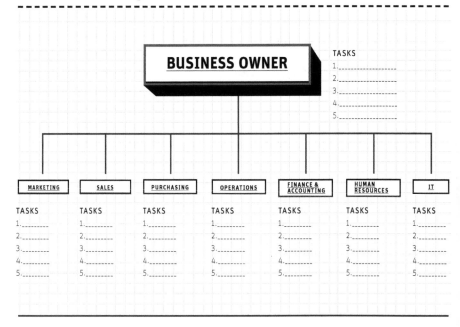

Creating a Functional Organizational Chart at Chicago Center Dentistry

"Although I have been practicing dentistry for nearly 30 years, I knew that something was missing in the way I assessed my operations and set my goals. With David's help, I was able to better focus and define my goals. David's guidance in the analysis of our previous years' performances helped us evaluate where we should concentrate our efforts to reach our objectives. His systematic approach to the analysis of our systems enabled our team to truly understand our operations and how our tasks are interrelated. I especially liked the way my entire staff was involved and energized."

— *Steve Fishman, Chicago Center Dentistry*

Tool #4: The System of Work Diagram

W hat is the overall system of your business?

Create a System of Work Diagram showing the whole-system of the business and key interfaces. This becomes the foundation for developing procedures, work instructions and forms.

Successful organizations are led and operated in a systematic and visible manner. By viewing workflow as a process, employees develop a shared understanding of how work flows through the system.

The System of Work Diagram provides the framework that shows employees where they fit into the business and how their individual actions may influence the company's overall performance.

The System of Work Diagram

- -

SUPPORT FUNCTIONS

FINANCE & ACCOUNTING	HUMAN RESOURCES	IT

"For the past couple of years I have had the pleasure of conducting audits for clients of David T. Lord. His approach to managing and collaborating with clients to develop and document their business processes is unique and refreshing.

David is a team coach who encourages open and creative thought resulting in a "System of Work." This is a unique, visually based, strategic tool that applies structure and color-coding to overall documentation and data analysis. I, along with David's clients, find the system to be a user-friendly approach to process documentation and process management.

Having conducted more than 400 audits, I have had the opportunity to view many approaches to consulting. As such, I can recommend only a very few consultants. David T. Lord is one of these."

— *David G. Attridge, Deloitte & Touche Quality Registrar Inc.*

A Completed System of Work

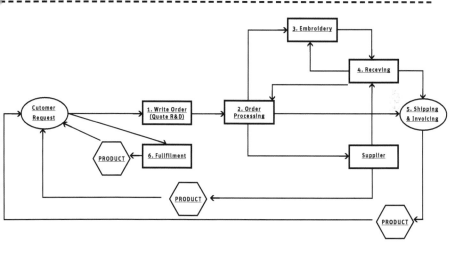

The Following Element does not apply:
- 7.3 Design and Development (all sub-elements)
- 7.6 Control of Nonconforming Material (all sub-elements)

Approval: _____ Date: _____

Tool #5: The Meeting Matrix Sheet

Developing a good meeting rhythm in your business allows you to use a series of meetings to build upon. This allows employees to see patterns that help them make better and faster decisions. Listed below are meetings that will help your business get into a rhythm:

Annual Meeting – review last year's goals, set and get alignment among your management team around this year's plan.

Quarterly Meetings – measuring progress toward your year-end goals and discuss what you need to do in the coming quarter.

Monthly Meetings – review progress with everyone, discuss financial results, and make appropriate adjustments. Focus on monthly objectives.

Weekly and Daily Huddles – these are 5-15 minute stand-up meetings for everyone. Use them to ensure everyone is focused on the right activities and identify interferences that may prevent the effectiveness or completion of a task/project.

Complete a Meeting Matrix Sheet to ensure meetings are structured with the right agenda that requires participation for employees to work together to make the business work better.

The Meeting Matrix Sheet

WHAT	WHY	WHEN	WHO	KEY REPORTS
1. ANNUAL STRATEGIC PLANNING SESSION				
2. ALL EMPLOYEE QUARTERLY REVIEW MEETING				
MONTHLY				
3. BOARD MEETING				
4. SALES MEETING				
5. OPERATIONS MEETING				
6. FINANCIAL REVIEW MEETING				
BI-MONTHLY				
7. LEADERSHIP TEAM MEETING				
WEEKLY				
8. OPERATIONS MEETING				
DAILY HUDDLE				
9. OFFICE MEETING				

Create a participative and collaborative workplace by fostering communication, cooperation and coordination of effort between everyone in the business. Establish a meeting rhythm (Annual, Quarterly, Monthly, Weekly and Daily) to manage the achievement of business goals and priorities at the individual, interpersonal, and inter-group levels.

"David helped us define what was most important, then assisted in mapping our system of work. He gave us tools and taught us methods to manage our time and our projects. He facilitated team meetings effectively and eased us through the process of change and growth. David helped us develop a culture that allowed employees to grow in skills and confidence. This led to a synergistic power of teamwork that promoted growth and productivity resulting in improved profits."

— *Jim Green, President, Milton Manufacturing Company*

Tool #6: The (2) Time Management Sheets

These ensure that employees know what to do (tasks) and how much time is required to complete them. Managing the time of employees effectively is reaching a shared understanding on tasks and time allocation.

Complete the following (2) Time Management Sheets to ensure your employees are doing the right things at the right time effectively:

Task Matrix Sheet

TASK	DAILY	WEEKLY	MONTHLY	QUARTERLY	BACKUP PRIMARY	SECONDARY

Task Matrix Example

Task Matrix Sheet

Name: Becky

TASK	DAILY	WEEKLY	MONTHLY	QUARTERLY	BACKUP PRIMARY	SECONDARY
Fill out paperwork	X				Kaye	Dee
Prepare for annual client reviews	X				Kaye	Dee
Put together monthly e-newsletters		X			Dee	Kaye
Put together client binders			X		Kaye	Dee
New client Mind-Maps			X		Dee	Kaye
Maintain company website			X		Dee	Kaye
Maintain and organize internal website				X	Dee	Kaye
Enter account information into Morningstar			X		Dee	Kaye
Input information in Excel			X		Dee	Kaye
Scan paperwork into LaserFiche			X		Dee	Kaye
Put together CPA binders			X		Kaye	Dee

Time Matrix Sheet

TIME	MONDAY	TUESDAY	WEDNESDAY	THURSDAY	FRIDAY
7:00 AM					
7:30 AM					
8:00 AM					
8:30 AM					
9:00 AM					
9:30 AM					
10:00 AM					
10:30 AM					
11:00 AM					
11:30 AM					
12:00 PM					
12:30 PM					
1:00 PM					
1:30 PM					
2:00 PM					
2:30 PM					
3:00 PM					
3:30 PM					
4:00 PM					
4:30 PM					
5:00 PM					
5:30 PM					
6:00 PM					
6:30 PM					
7:00 PM					

Task Matrix Example

Time Matrix Sheet

TIME	MONDAY	TUESDAY	WEDNESDAY	THURSDAY	FRIDAY
7:00 AM			NOT IN THE OFFICE		
7:30 AM					
8:00 AM			WEEKLY STAFF MEETING	STRATEGIC PLANNING WITH STEPHEN	
8:30 AM					
9:00 AM	STRATEGIC PLANNING WITH STEPHEN	UPDATE PROSPECT REPORTS		UPDATE FINANCIAL REPORTS	CUSTOMER FOR LIFE REFERRAL FOR LIFE
9:30 AM					
10:00 AM		STEPHEN HUDDLE	STEPHEN HUDDLE	STEPHEN HUDDLE	STEPHEN HUDDLE
10:30 AM					
11:00 AM					
11:30 AM					
12:00 PM					
12:30 PM	LOAN STRUCTURING	LOAN STRUCTURING	LOAN STRUCTURING	LOAN STRUCTURING	LOAN STRUCTURING
1:00 PM	PROCESS MEETING	PROJECTS		PROJECTS	
1:30 PM					
2:00 PM					
2:30 PM					PROJECTS
3:00 PM					
3:30 PM					
4:00 PM		COMPLETE FCMs			
4:30 PM			PREPARE FOR NEXT DAY		
5:00 PM	STEPHEN HUDDLE	STEPHEN HUDDLE	STEPHEN HUDDLE	STEPHEN HUDDLE	STEPHEN HUDDLE
5:30 PM					
6:00 PM					
6:30 PM			NOT IN THE OFFICE		
7:00 PM					

Tool #7: The 5W-2H Worksheet

Because employees have different views...

"KEEP six honest serving-men
(They taught me all I knew);
Their names are What and Why and When
And How and Where and Who.
I send them over land and sea,
I send them east and west;
But after they have worked for me,
I give them all a rest."

— **Rudyard Kipling,** *an English short-story writer,*
poet, and novelist

In order to accomplish a project or run an effective meeting, completing a 5W-2H Work Sheet is a must! To complete any endeavor, the following questions must be answered:

What to do? (Subject)

Why do it? (Purpose)

When should it be done? (Sequence)

Where should it be done? (Location)

Who should do it? (People)

How should it be done? (Method)

How much should be done? (Time and Money)

Complete a 5W-2H Worksheet to manage projects effectively, to achieve 'on-time' and 'within budget' performance or to help run effective meetings.

The 5W-2H Worksheet

WHAT
(Subject/What To Do)

WHY
(Purpose)

WHEN
(Sequence)

WHERE
(Location)

WHO
(People)

HOW
(Method)

HOW MUCH
(Time/$)

The 5W-2H Project Example
Retain 100% of our Clients

WHAT

(Subject) What to do	Review Client retention process and revise to enable the company to retain 100% of our Clients.

WHY

(Purpose) Why do it	Retaining existing Clients while obtaining new Clients will make the business a profitable and successful company while also providing added value to the Client.

WHEN

(Sequence)	Specific dates will be tied to each "How"

WHERE

(Location)	Corporate Office and onsite with Clients

WHO

(People)	Leadership Team and Account Management Team

HOW

(Method) Required Action Items	**INTERNAL** 1) Define Client success and failure by developing and analyzing a snapshot spreadsheet of all Clients **EMPLOYER** 1) Ask all Clients the 3 Questions 2) Research CFO requirements to approve Health Promotion Program 3) Create an Exit Survey **EMPLOYEE** 1) Analyze employee survey results for satisfaction and feedback 2) Review Usage Data 3) Review Gap Analysis for employee comprehension

HOW MUCH

(Time/$)	No Cost

The 5W-2H Agenda Example
Executive Council Meeting

WHAT: 1st Executive Council Meeting

WHY: To reach consensus on what's most important to accomplish over the next 6-8 weeks.

WHEN: May 16, 2012, 2:00-4:00 PM

WHO: Richard, Bob, Betty and Pat

HOW: Agenda

1. Meeting purpose and desire outcomes

2. The importance of having TRUST for one another

3. The Key Outcome of the Developing a Quality Culture Meeting
a. The need for a Family Succession Plan
b. The need for an Organization Structure
c. Feedback for moving forward

4. Key Action Items for Moving Forward
a. Calculate required monthly throughput to achieve breakeven
b. Create a visual method to track and monitor 'Hot Jobs' and Open Orders/Backlog.
c. Discover how to overcome the key constraints that prevent on-time delivery (incoming material and the CNC machines).
d. Improve the Bill of Material (BOM) quality.
e. Create an action plan to prepare for the next 4-6 months forecasted demand.
f. Prioritize the 'Wish List' for the five divisions (staffing and equipment).
g. Develop a Scoreboard (Performance Metrics).

5. Determine next steps

Tool #8: The Scoreboard

Your company should have a scoreboard to measure its progress in relation to the business objectives. Like watching a sporting event, monitoring the company's scoreboard lets employees understand how they are doing.

Your business needs to track and monitor the Lag and Lead measures to improve business performance. Employees need to know what results are needed each day, week and month to achieve the desired results.

A highly visual scoreboard promotes immediate, constant feedback and accountability. Keeping everyone informed on how the business is performing lets employees know if they are winning or losing and what adjustments are needed to improve business performance.

Create a Scoreboard Sheet to show which Lag and Lead measures will have the greatest impact on making money and generating cash.

THE SCOREBOARD SHEET

NET PROFIT	CASH FLOW

THROUGHPUT (SALES)	OPERATING EXPENSES

RATE OF WORKFLOW	QUALITY ISSUES/CONCERNS

ACCOUNTS RECEIVABLE (A/R)	ACCOUNTS PAYABLE (A/P)

THE SCOREBOARD SHEET EXAMPLE

----

1. EMPLOYEE SATISFACTION

Job Clarity? 6/10
Up to date employee tools? 9/10
Appropriate job for strengths? 7/10
Quarterly Bonuses Paid? YES
Employee Recognition? 3/10
Annual Employee Party? YES
Non Work Events? 2/10
Health Insurance? NO
Retirement Benefits? NO

2. QUOTES & TECHNOLOGY ROADMAPS

8 customer meetings per month?
$40,000 in quotes per month?
Average $57,000 per month?
Measure our closing rate for quotes: NOT YET
Average 4 Technology Road Maps per month: O

3. CUSTOMER SATISFACTION (CUSTOMER COMPAINTS)

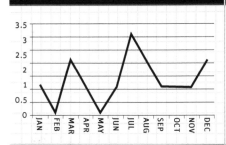

4. THROUGHPUT (BILLABLE HOURS): GOAL 350 HOURS

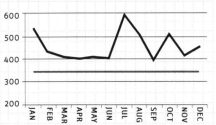

5. TICKETS CLOSED PER MONTH

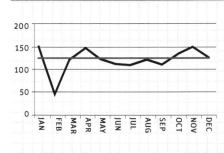

6. OPERATING EXPENSES BETWEEN $27.5 & $42.5K

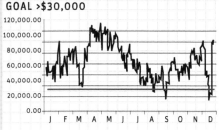

7. NET PROFIT: GOAL $196,000/YEAR

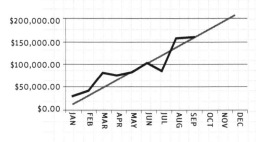

8. CASH FLOW (BANK ACCOUNT BALANCE) GOAL >$30,000

The scoreboard provides a snapshot of the business and is essential in decision making. What areas are doing well? Which need help? Sound decisions are based on facts. The measures you have in place need to be used and reviewed to make the business better. Keeping score will help keep your business accountable.

"David introduced our team to visual management. Seeing data is critical to the success of any organization. In today's technology-driven marketplace, where critical pieces of data and reports reside in someone's inbox or intranet site, David Lord knows that the only way to truly interpret the results of your work as a team is through visual management. Perhaps David's most important contribution to Leedo was his implementation of storyboards, a tool that helps people visualize processes, responsibilities, schedules and measurements. Storyboards have allowed us to effectively review our results as a group and discuss continual improvement opportunities."

— *Trey Dudley, Director of Installation Services, Leedo*

Chapter
07
Getting Better in 90 Days

"Great things are not done by impulse, but by a series of small things brought together."

— *Vincent Van Gogh,* *Dutch post-Impressionist painter whose work had a far-reaching influence on 20th-century art*

07

GETTING BETTER IN 90 DAYS

Implementing a Throughput Improvement Plan

As noted in Chapter 5, if a small business wants to prosper, it has to make money and generate cash. It can accomplish this by saving money or making money. Progressive business owners focus on making money by increasing throughput.

In order to change to an "increasing throughput" method of working, a business can utilize an uncomplicated and effective process, the Throughput Improvement Plan (TIP). When managing workflow, there is a leverage point that will have the greatest impact to help a business make money and generate cash. A TIP helps to select a leverage point (constraint) and identify the "interferences" that slow down or stop the flow of work from doing more and/or doing better.

The TIP process communicates to employees the role they must play to help increase the rate of workflow at the constraint. It is a common-sense way of including everyone in genuine productivity improvement. A TIP creates unity within the organization and increases the rate of workflow. That, far more than cutting costs, helps small businesses make money and generate cash. At little or no increase in operating expenses, TIP will deliver the benefits of increased throughput while improving quality and on-time delivery.

A Chain is only as Strong as its Weakest Link

"It is a mistake to look too far ahead. Only one link in the chain of destiny can be handled at a time."

— Winston Churchill, *British politician, best known for his leadership of the United Kingdom during the Second World War*

The weakest link in a business is called a "constraint." A constraint is the part of the system that is most likely to impose delays everywhere else in the system. The constraint dictates the rhythm of the pace of workflow in the system.

A business can only be as strong as its weakest link. Your business's constraints affect how much your business can improve. In order to help your business work better, it is critical to identify its weakest link, the constraint.

INPUT → [20] [16] [10] [14] [18] → OUTPUT (T)

↑ CONSTRAINT

MAX OUTPUT = 10 (FOR ONE HOUR)

☐ PROCESS STEPS ⬡ UNITS ⏱ TIME T THROUGHPUT

07

The 7-Step Process for Improving Throughput Performance

The biggest obstacle to solving a problem is to first be able to define the problem. It is difficult to determine the correct solution if you are not sure what problem you are trying to solve. TIP offers a simple and powerful process for selecting and exploiting workflow constraints. Employees closely associated with the selected constraint become the experts to identify what interferences are responsible for the constraint. Those employees are asked the following question:

What are the constraint "interferences" that slow down or stop the flow of work from doing more and/or doing better?

The answers to the question become the list of "interferences," the reasons "why" the constraint cannot do more or better. To get more from the constraint, the interferences must be reduced or removed completely.

Listed below are the seven steps that a business can take to discover where to focus resources to get the biggest leverage for the company to make money and generate cash:

Step 1 – Select the workflow constraint

Step 2 – Identify the interferences of the constraint

Step 3 – Quantify and prioritize the interferences

Step 4 – Select what interference should be solved first

Step 5 – Decide what must exist so the selected interference is reduced or removed completely

Step 6 – Implement the interference 'reduction or removal' action plans.

Step 7 – Verify action plan effectiveness

Increase THROUGHPUT by doing more work faster and better at the selected workflow constraint.

The power of selecting and exploiting workflow constraints is that it will dramatically increase throughput of a business, which means making more money and generating more cash.

07

The Discipline for Improving Throughput Performance

"You'll never plough a field turning it over in your mind."

— *Irish Proverb*

Looking at the business through different key perspectives is critical. The (8) tools can exist alone or unite to create distinct mixtures. This foundation allows a small business owner to fine tune business improvement methods to meet clients' needs. This structured process must also allow for the flexibility that each individual business will need.

The 90 Day Implementation Plan (see the diagram on page 89) utilizes the (8) tools and focuses on four disciplines for making money and generating cash:

1. Focus. Remarkable results can be achieved when your employees are clear about what's most important. Identify where to leverage your organization by selecting the constraints that will have the greatest impact on increasing Throughput for the business.

2. Leverage. Act on the constraints and Lead measures.

3. Engagement. Engage all employees by creating a compelling scoreboard for the constraints and Lead measures, showing whether the business is winning or losing.

4. Accountability. Create accountability by establishing a rhythm of frequent and regular meetings that address the constraints and Lead measures.

90 Day Implementation Plan

STEP	ACTIVITY	IMPLEMENTATION DESCRIPTION	THE (8) TOOLS IN ACTION	WEEKS (1 2 3 4 5 6 7 8 9 10 11 12)
01	INTRODUCTION	THE METHOD AND TOOLS/ PROJECT PLAN	7	■ (wk 1)
02	BUILD THE FOUNDATION	STRATEGIC/ORGANIZATION/ FINANCIAL	1-2-3	■ (wk 2)
03	PREPARE FOR THE PROJECT	SYSTEM OF WORK/COMMAND CENTER/SCOREBOARD	4-8	■ (wk 2)
04	COMPANY KICK-OFF	INTRODUCE EMPLOYEES TO 90 DAY ACTION PLAN	7	■ (wk 3)
05	CONDUCT TIP TRAINING	INTRODUCE EMPLOYEES TO TIP PROCESS	7	■ (wk 3)
06	LINK TEAMS	DEVELOP THE KEY MEETING MATRIX	5	■ (wk 4)
07	MONTHLY REVIEW #1	MANAGEMENT TEAM REVIEWS STATUS OF PROJECT	7	■ (wk 4) ■ (wk 6)
08	BEGIN MEETING RHYTHM	KICK-OFF WEEKLY MEETINGS AND DAILY HUDDLES	5-7	▬▬▬▬ (wks 5-12)
09	INTRO PROJECT MGT	INSTITUTE PROJECT MANAGEMENT DISCIPLINE	7	▬▬▬ (wks 6-11)
10	INTRO TIME MGT	DEVELOP TASK/REPORT/MEETING/ TIME MATRICIES	6	▬▬▬ (wks 6-11)
11	TIP PROJECT (40 DAYS)	IMPLEMENT THROUGHPUT IMPROVEMENT PLAN #1	3-4-5-6-7-8	▬▬▬ (wks 6-12)
12	QUARTERLY REVIEW #1	CONDUCT QUARTERLY REVIEW/ 3-MONTH OBJECTIVES	1-2-3-4-5-7-8	▬ (wk 12)

07

Roque Pena completing a "Transition Action Plan" with timeline

"The Visual System of Work will engage small business owners to think differently on how to manage their daily, weekly and monthly activities to continually improve their operation."

— *Roque Pena Jr., Friend and Mentoree*

Projects are Important

"Projects are the lifeblood of most organizations; not just project-based such as construction and software companies. Product development is a project. Productivity improvements are projects. Business acquisitions are projects. Market development efforts are projects. Every single strategic component of the enterprise is a project. Thus, the economic health of the organization rests on the organization's ability to conceive, plan and execute projects successfully. Projects are where the money is because of the value to the organization they add."

— **Mark J. Woeppel,** founder and President of Pinnacle Strategies International and author of *Projects in Less Time*

Conclusion

Cn

Call to Action

"The future will depend on what we do in the present."

— *Mahatma Gandhi,* preeminent leader of Indian nationalism in British-ruled India, who led India to independence and inspired movements for non-violence, civil rights and freedom across the world

Cn

CONCLUSION

Call to Action

"Nike's golden slogan resonates with the wisdom of psychoanalysis: just do it! Indeed, we all need that kind of urging at critical points in our lives when we are faced with fear and indecision, at the crossroads of the same—old—same—old and the new venture. Call it cutting the cord, taking the plunge, carpe—ing the Diem. Sometimes we just have to screw up our courage and take the leap of faith."

— Jennifer Kunst, Ph.D., a clinical psychologist and psychoanalyst who works with adults and couples in her private practice in Pasadena, CA

O ver the next 90 days, your business will experience an exciting new era of achievement and success. You now have the ingeniously simple method and tools you need to bring your business into a new period of growth and accomplishment. You cannot change the past, but you can make a fresh start that will lead your organization to a new, victorious ending. By using the Visual System of Work, your business will soon be working better, making more money and generating more cash.

Your business is a complex structure. Begin, now, to use these easy visualization methods to better understand the scope of how your business actually works. Put information about your business on storyboards and let everybody see its fundamental structure. Use the simple forms I have given you. Identify where the leverage points are, implement a TIP, watch the scoreboard and organize a meeting rhythm. These are simple acts that will get everyone personally involved. Soon, your employees will be working together, communicating with each other and coordinating their efforts in a spirit of confidence and cooperation.

And, suddenly, you will notice that your business has begun to transform.

Your people are your greatest assets. Together, they either already have the answers, or else they will use their collective, creative spark to find them. When employees are able to see how a business truly works, what their part is in it, and how the different parts interconnect, they naturally start to work together as a cohesive unit. You'll notice the energy in your organization is different. Your employees will be feeling more empowered, optimistic, helpful and encouraged. Your customers and suppliers will also be happier because problems will be managed regularly and proactively and transactions will be more organized, effective and reliable.

There is no limit to the success you and your business can achieve by using the Visual System of Work. Make the decision to begin now. Take step one and then continue to follow the method and use the tools. I know you can do it! The future is in your hands.

Cn

Summary

"Lacking systems or not following the ones in place creates extra work, wastes time and money. Also makes work hell."

— *Text message received April 2008*

1. MONEY IS CREATED BY WORK.

2. A SYSTEM OF WORK IS HOW A BUSINESS MAKES MONEY AND GENERATES CASH.

3. THROUGHPUT, TRUE VARIABLE COSTS, AND OPERATING EXPENSES ARE THE KEY LEAD MEASURES FOR MANAGING THE SYSTEM OF WORK.

4. THROUGHPUT IMPROVEMENT PLAN (TIP) IDENTIFIES CONSTRAINTS WITHIN THE SYSTEM OF WORK THAT WILL GIVE THE GREATEST LEVERAGE FOR IMPROVING BUSINESS PERFORMANCE.

5. PROCESS AND PEOPLE CAPABILITY AND THE CAPACITY WITHIN THE BUSINESS PROCESSES TO MANAGE THE CONSTRAINTS WILL HAVE THE GREATEST IMPACT MAKING MONEY AND GENERATING CASH FOR THE BUSINESS.

6. PEOPLE ARE THE GREATEST ASSET OF A BUSINESS.

7. BUSINESS LEADERSHIP DETERMINES HOW SUCCESSFUL A BUSINESS WILL BECOME.

"Learning organizations [are] organizations where people continually expand their capacity to create the results they truly desire, where new and expansive patterns of thinking are nurtured, where collective aspiration is set free, and where people are continually learning to see the whole together."

—**Peter Senge,** *American scientist and director of the Center for Organizational Learning at the MIT Sloan School of Management*

Kudos for David T. Lord and the Book

"Business leaders who want to make more money and improve their business will greatly benefit from "The Visual System of Work." Don't let the thinness of the spine fool you. I found this quick motivating read clearly lays out the key steps to accelerate business improvement. I have had the privilege of seeing David in action as he successfully implemented the methods in this book for a family owned business and for units of a Fortune 100 business. Both made more money and developed cohesive, engaged, high-performing management teams. Pass out this book to your management team. Start up a study/action group and watch your business improve."

— *Linda Hogan, Performance Improvement Consultant*

"David Lord has distilled in this book his quarter-century experience helping small businesses. There are many good suggestions that you can follow, and if you still have questions, why not give him a call."

— *David J. Lu, retired Professor emeritus, Bucknell University and translator of What is Quality Control? By Kaoru Ishikawa and author of The Dawn of History to the Late Tokugawa Period (Japan - A Documentary History)*

"David helped us define what was most important, then assisted in mapping our system of work. He gave us tools and taught us methods to manage our time and our projects. He facilitated team meetings effectively and eased us through the process of change and growth. David helped us develop a culture that allowed employees to grow in skills and confidence. This led to a synergistic power of teamwork that promoted growth and productivity resulting in improved profits."

— *Jim Green, President, Milton Manufacturing Company*

"During the time that David worked with the Taylor Group, he introduced the following three tools: System of Work, which mapped our processes, identified constraints and created a method for tracking and monitoring work flow; Task Matrix Management, which helped employees understand roles and responsibilities in relation to the System of Work and 5W-2H Project Management, which helped us organize and complete projects on time. David facilitated meetings and asked the right questions enabling us to extract and analyze pertinent information to diagnose constraints within our System of Work. David's enthusiastic way of getting people motivated and his method and tools have improved our performance throughout the entire company."

— *Jim Taylor, President, Taylor Group Insurance*

Kudos for David T. Lord and the Book

I realized quickly that David had a unique ability to see and comprehend complex issues and to distill them into clear and understandable visual maps. We knew as a team that although we had strong leaders, we were not always communicating as effectively and fully as possible. Through the development of visual maps for the different business areas, everyone on the leadership team, and subsequently in the business groups, now have a more clear understanding of our work flow."

— *Joe Hart, President, Asset Health*

"Leedo was struggling as a manufacturer and turn-key solution in the multifamily cabinet industry. David worked with our manufacturing team to establish control over our system. Various plant teams mapped workflow, identified critical handoffs, developed dashboards and established employee responsibilities. Mindsets were changed which drove the mantra of accountability at the most basic level. The results were truly astounding. Manufacturing began to fill orders on-time and became the stalwart to the organization."

— *David Burke, VP Sales Administration, Leedo Cabinetry*

"I had the privilege of working with David as we implemented his visual system for a $560M organization culminating in improved performance, employee empowerment, customer satisfaction, and public quality awards. This succinct book is packed with the very approach and tools David used to guide us through that transformation. Even more importantly, David's personal value of data integrity and transparency resonates on every page."

— *Don Springer, President and CEO of the Colton Group*

"The Visual System of Work will engage small business owners to think differently on how to manage their daily, weekly and monthly activities to continually improve their operation. This book provides the essential tools every small business owner needs to get organized, getting everyone involved to become part of the ultimate goal: increase throughput and generate cash. David's concepts can also be very valuable for management teams needing goal alignment within a corporation. The Eight Tools are basic guidelines company leaders can take and develop as their own to manage and continually improve an operation."

—*Roque Pena Jr., Friend and Mentoree*

Kudos for David T. Lord and the Book

"David has a masterfully visual mind that allows him to see the business process in a very organized way. We found through our work that we had many of the pieces but we needed to organize and document them into a System of Work. We found that things became so much clearer when they were documented on paper. That process alone causes one to evaluate the process to see that it makes sense or possibly may need to be modified. Our organization is better off because of the work of David Lord."

— Thomas A. Trumbull, President, Suburban Aviation

"Without question, David became an active consultant and inspirational leader for our management team guiding, educating and motivating us to understand and commit to the key fundamentals of enhancing our work flow and service delivery process. He advised me in establishing a framework for management training workshops and facilitating a process to re-invigorate our team's commitment to our vision, mission and core values.

Most importantly, we successfully reached consensus on a workflow process to insure enhanced communication, effective planning, hand-offs and service delivery with on-time, complete and accurate delivery of our health screening services. I especially appreciated David's personal commitment to me and his role as advisor and mentor. He consistently communicated and supported me with information, ideas and sample planning tools to adjust to unplanned "whirlwind" and helped us reach our goals."

— Charles B. Estey, President, Health Solutions

"Those who advise business owners and leaders should never presume the fundamentals are clearly understood. This book will be a way for owners and leaders to put structure to their intuition about important business issues. Congratulations on a wonderful book. Your clarity of thought is impressive. All the best."

— Michael Kioc, Chief Financial Officer, RHK Technology

"Having worked (personally) with David on projects using this method and tools; the outcomes were very successful. David has a unique way of getting things done and achieving goals. This book is a good capture of David's use of the overall process."

— Charles B. Dygert, professor, motivational speaker and author of Creating a Culture of Success: Fine-Tuning the Heart and Soul of Your Organization

Acknowledgements

Certain individuals have made a tremendous impact on my life, which has helped develop the ideas, subject matter and content of this book. Listed below are the names of my mentors:

Henry Cisco	*Gordon Belt*	*Edgar H. Schein*
Violet Cisco	*Larry Sullivan*	*Don Springer*
Tracy Lord	*Gordon Keefe*	*Jerry McNellis*
Connie Lord	*Charles B. Dygert*	*Paul Henderson*
Vic Lawson	*David J. Lu*	*Robert E. Fox*

And… These are the names of my confidants who have supported me over the years:

Mike Angerer	*Mike Kloc*	*Anthony Roark*
Joel Banda	*Phil Laure*	*Mark Ryan*
David Burke	*Robert Lemon*	*Craig Schrotenboer*
Trey Dudley	*Adam T. Lord*	*Ed Stines*
Anthony O. Giorgio	*James P. Millett*	*Bob Sullivan*
Jim Green Jr.	*Bob Moesta*	*James Taylor*
Joe Hart	*Roque Pena*	*John (JT) Taylor*
Linda Hogan	*Phil Rice*	*Gregory B. Williams*

I want to thank Joshua Smith and Jessica Janda for utilizing their talents to make the book come alive through book design and artistic presentation.

I want to thank Jerry Hutchinson for his dynamic cover design.

I want to thank my daughter, Mariah C. Taylor and my son, Adam T. Lord for their on-going support and encouragement for completing the book.

Most of all, I want to thank my wife, Lolo A. Lord, for the masterful job she performed in editing this book. Until the words made sense on paper, the ideas, subject matter and content of this book would have been meaningless.

About the Author

David T. Lord is a business consultant, coach and facilitator with over 25 years of experience working with businesses of all types and sizes. David knows how to make businesses effective by identifying processes that need improvement, then helping to make those improvements a reality. Over 100 business owners and leaders with their team members have found utilizing David's tools timeless and continue their journey today. His approach will show you how to develop a business culture that is committed to employees, pleasing to the customer and continuously improving.

Disclaimer

This book is designed to provide information on helping a business get better. It is sold with the understanding that the author is not engaged in rendering legal, accounting or other professional services. If legal or other expert assistance is required, the services of a competent professional should be sought.

It is not the purpose of this book to reprint all the information that is otherwise available to authors and/or publishers, but instead to complement, amplify, and supplement other texts. You are urged to read all the available material, learn as much as possible and tailor the information to your individual needs.

Every effort has been made to make this book as complete and as accurate as possible. However, there may be mistakes, both typographical and in content. Therefore, this text should be used only as a general guide and not the ultimate source of information. Furthermore, this book contains information that is current only up to the printing date.

The purpose of this book is to educate. The author shall have neither liability nor responsibility to any person or entity with any loss or damage caused, or alleged to have been caused, directly or indirectly, by the information contained in this book.

IF YOU DO NOT WISH TO BE BOUND BY THE ABOVE, YOU MAY RETURN THIS BOOK TO THE AUTHOR FOR A FULL REFUND WITH PROOF OF PURCHASE WITHIN 90 DAYS.

VISUAL SYSTEM OF WORK

Help Your Business Work Better,
Make Money and Generate Cash:
A 90 Day Implementation Guide

QUICK ORDER FORM

To order your copy of this book, compete this form and mail to:

David T. Lord Consulting, LLC
PO Box 971334
Ypsilanti, MI 48197

Your Name
_____

Address
_____

City/State/Zip
_____

Telephone/Date
_____

Signature
_____

PAYMENT make checks payable to **David T. Lord Consulting, LLC**

Number of Books:	**14.95 per copy**	$
Shipping & Handling	**$5 per order**	$
Tax [residents of Michigan only] **6%**		$

Check   CC

Card Number
_____

Name/Expiration date
_____

davidtlord
helping your business work better

David T. Lord Consulting, LLC
www.davidtlord.com
☎ 866-375-3281

"For I know the plans I have for you,"
declares the Lord, "plans to
prosper you and not to harm you,
plans to give you hope and a future."

— *Jeremiah 29:11*